Whispers of the Soul

Dr. Mallika Tripathi

BookLeaf Publishing

India | USA | UK

Presentation by *BookLeaf Publishing*

Web: www.bookleafpub.com

E-mail: info@bookleafpub.com

ISBN: 9789363310506

First edition 2024

ACKNOWLEDGEMENT

This book would not have been possible without the unwavering support and encouragement of several special people in my life.

First and foremost, to my soulmate, Vishal —your love and faith in me have been the bedrock of my journey. Your constant support has given me the strength to pursue my passion for poetry and share it with the world.

To my son, Mahaveer—you are my inspiration and my joy. Your curiosity and wonder remind me daily of the beauty in life's simplest moments. Thank you for filling my days with laughter and love.

To my family and friends—you have been my confidants, my critics, and my cheerleaders. Your insights, encouragement, and unwavering support have been invaluable. Thank you for believing in my vision and for always being there to share my successes and challenges.

To my publisher—your guidance, patience, and expertise have brought this collection to life.

Thank you for believing in this project and for your dedication to bringing "Whispers of the Soul" to readers everywhere.

All of you have played a vital role in this journey, and for that, I am profoundly grateful. This book is a testament to the power of love, friendship, and collaboration. Thank you from the bottom of my heart.

With deepest gratitude,

Dr. Mallika Tripathi

PREFACE

In the quiet moments between the rush of daily life and the solitude of night, poetry finds its place. It is in these moments that "Whispers of the Soul" was born—a collection that seeks to capture the ephemeral yet profound experiences that define our human existence.

This anthology is a journey through the heart's most intimate corridors and the mind's vast landscapes. It is a reflection on love in its myriad forms, from the passionate to the platonic, the fleeting to the enduring. Here, you will find poems that celebrate love's beauty and complexity, revealing the delicate balance between joy and sorrow that it often brings.

Life, with all its unpredictability, is another central theme of this collection. The poems herein explore the highs and lows, the mundane and the extraordinary, painting a vivid picture of the human experience. They invite you to pause and reflect on the moments that shape us, the choices we make, and the paths we tread.

Society and values are threads woven throughout this tapestry of verse. These poems question the norms, challenge the status quo, and ponder the principles that guide our lives. They offer a mirror to our collective conscience, encouraging introspection

Warrior

I am a born fighter,
Freedom is my right.
Sailing beyond confinements,
I know no boundaries,
Though I never fought any battle,
But the spirit of a warrior dwells within me.
Sometimes I fight with my inner self,
That asks me to be the part of cowards,
But I resist and protest,
And emerge victorious.
Winning over all my follies,
I crave for freedom of soul
In this ephemeral world
That is bound to perish.
Whether you are a millionaire or billionaire,
It matters not,
For once you leave for the eternal abode,
Just the ashes remain, scribbling your deeds.

Abode of Eternity

Living beyond religion is the toughest task,
I am born witnessing the hatred around,
Everyone fighting over trivial issues,
The issues of Hindu and Musalmaan,
Their souls heavily chained,
Failing to bear the weight of black iron,
I remain dumb among an army of extremists,
They are learned people,
Have read many scriptures and Quran
I can't touch them, they stand tall,
I feel confused over the entire episode,
What is this fight for?
Who stands behind this bloodshed?
Killing the spirit of humanity,
Who will win; a Hindu or Muslim,
Finally the cries of lamenting crowd,
Will not be borne by both,
The mourning will become eternal.
I open my eyes to see if someone is alive,

My people who have become the epitome of
cruelty,
They talk so much about womanhood,
Yet the sound of brotherhood gets lost,
The very day a woman is raped,
And the talks of womanhood get wrapped.
I wish to ask them,
Do rapists have any religion?
Do the sufferings of Hindus and Muslims differ?
I know they won't answer,
They are destined to follow the blind mob,
But I know no religion,
For I am a Teacher.
I don't differentiate among my pupils;
I treat them as equals,
They are an indispensable part of my life,
Irrespective of their caste, creed, or color,
They touch my soul,
Living forever in my memory,
They strive to achieve their goals,
I feel content and close my eyes,
Chasing the road of sanctity,
I yearn to dwell in the abode of eternity.

Divine Flame

As I rest in nature's embrace, watching the drops
of dew,
In the moonbeams' glow, hope blooms anew.
Easing hermitic burdens, it dissipates all stress,
Healing tormented souls, restoring blessedness.
Ecstasy reigns supreme, a gentle breeze,
In tranquil minds where laurels find ease.
Elderly dream of joyous twilight years,
Filled with laughter where the cool wind clears.
Senses satisfied by sweet scents' allure,
A serene heaven, a tranquiliser pure.
Blessed with peace and opulence, an ethereal
dance,
Festivities flourish, in nature's radiant expanse.
Amidst buoyant spirits, whispers soft and near,
Secret mantras of joy, the heart holds dear.
'Keep the Divine flame alive forever', they say,
Thankful for nature's protection, angelic each
day.
In nature's embrace, we find solace profound,
Her nurturing touch, a symphony of sound.

From moonbeam to breeze, from scent to sight,
She paints serenity with colors bright.
Grateful hearts sing praises, humble and true,
To mother nature, protector, ever anew.

Heavenly Abode

My soul left for the heavenly abode,
Yearning to unite with the unknown,
On the way to my eternal dwelling,
I saw people mourning,
As funeral replaced all the fun and frolic,
It left everyone quite melancholic,
There was a lot of chaos,
To burn the body before it deteriorated,
Everyone appeared vacuous as if inebriated.
A lovely daughter; doting wife,
Mother of two adorable children,
I lived all my relations,
Fulfilling all my duties,
I never expected more from life,
But before I could come out of my sweet
slumber,
I became a body; a body to be burnt on pyre,
Else it would stink to pollute the environment.
My love, dedication and sacrifice, all in vain,
It was too disheartening to see people lamenting,
And suddenly getting back to their normal
course of life,
I no longer existed for them,
Those who had been the reason for my
existence.

Broken, I looked up at the sky,
To hear the symphony,
It gave me some solace,
I regretted not performing my last ritual,
The ritual of saying the last words,
I silently murmured,
'Let my soul be eternally united with you, my
Lord!'

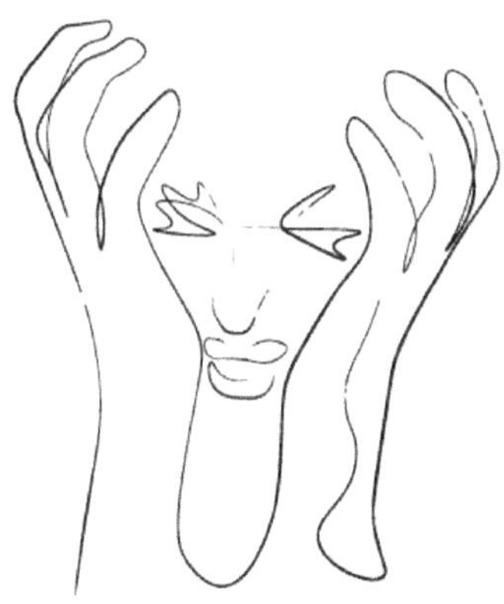

Pink

Pink, the color of love,
Lost its meaning over time,
With references to the fairer sex,
It became the symbol of subordination.
Having its roots in the patriarchal society,
Unknowingly, blue became the ruling monarch.
The romance between the two faded,
As the latter inclined to dominate the former.
Blue no more felt the passion or the fire,
But decided to let the pink down.
It created a gap; a gap that could never be bridged,
They became like two opposite poles,
Resolute not to meet again.
There started a war—the war between the blue and pink,
As the pink decided to revolt,
To get carte blanche from age-old bondage,

To be a free spirit again,
It annoyed the blue and it got adamant to
avenge,
The balance between the two was drastically
disturbed,
Affecting all that existed on Earth,
The earth became the battleground; bleeding and
sobbing,
People failed to express the gory details,
None could escape the fury,
The dumb spectators looked up to the sky,
They cried to quash an unending battle.
Hearing the prayers,
A dim flickering light showed the way,
The way to peace; to eternity,
The dark ended for a dawn,
Now the pink became the Empress
To avenge the cause and to lead an opulent life.
The blue was arrested to be tormented,
And the pink decided to govern and rule,
But to others' surprise,
It was not the head but the heart of the blue.

I am a Woman

I am a woman of today; fierce, fiery and violent,
Taking control of my life, I am no more a
parasite,
Educated, independent, I walk my own way.

I am audacious enough to challenge the wrong,
Virtuous and simple but not naive,
I can't be fooled in the name of customs,
I am not blindfolded; I see what goes around.

I raise my voice against all evils,
I am no more a quaking creature,
I refuse to be enslaved in this patriarchal society,
I am full of questions; ready to save my
existence,
I am no more a stock of laughter, rather I save
others from being ridiculed,
I detest those who try to teach me the proper
dress code or to be submissive.

Gone are the days when I surrendered like a
coward,
Now I am ready to fight—not the people but the
devilish thoughts,

That kept me confined within the four walls for
centuries,
I am neither scared of the dirty looks nor the
lewd remarks,
You can't snatch my dignity,
I'll pay back in the same coin; if you ever dare
to hurt my soul.

I'll not wait for the justice to be served
But I will hang you myself till death without any
further delay,
I'll no longer beg for succor but I'll choose my
own way.
I am followed not because of my stunning
presence,
But because of my strength,
I can't be defeated; my soul remains invincible.

I neither wish to lead nor wish to follow
But I just wish you to stand by my side,
To create a world where women can live a
dignified life,
Without any fear of being raped or victimised,
Where they are not judged by their attire
But by their attitude towards life,
Where their flesh is not sold
But they are revered as the creators,
Where they are not confined within the scary
cells

But are given the wings of imagination to fly
high in the sky,
Where people might forget to celebrate the
Women's Day,
But all remain committed to ceasing the female
feticide...

Palghar's Tragedy

I saw a frail, simple saint,
Trembling, terrified, crying for help,
He looked miserable,
Holding the hands of a custodian,
He was horrified like a child,
But the protector himself threw him
In front of the bloodthirsty vampires,
Who were ready to suck his blood,
He ran here and there to save his life but all in
vain,
The entire sight was gruesome.
Being agonised he mistook the venomous
monster to be a saviour,
Who not only deceived him but handed him over
to the barbarians,

Humanity was beaten to death...
But no one came to rescue,
Is it the same India that we dreamt of?
Where the sacred have to pay the cost for
wearing saffron,
The dumb spectators relished the gory,
And the ruling befooled the fools,
I was dumbstruck to see the brutality,
Forced to pass the sleepless nights,
My soul cursed the wicked,
But the cruel reality could never be changed
The big-hearted was beheaded
Giving rise to a contentious discussion...

An Apology

My apologies for disappointing you, my love!
Trust me, you are my little, pure and holy dove.
Today I'll be apart due to my duty call,
But you always inspire me to be victorious even
after facing a squall.

You are my love and my pride,
The only ray of hope, left in my life.
You are the true mensch for whom my heart
beats,
And I'll heartily feel the distance and scorching
heat.

Though it's hard to endure this pain,
But I stand strong to wait for the rain.
As I often see the Almighty in your disguise,
Hence I feel blessed to be your choice.

Invincible

Even the darkness failed to darken my Soul,
I still feel optimistic for a glorious dawn,
No one can ever subjugate me,
Who could ever control the thunder and storm?

I may give all for the sake of love,
But not otherwise,
So don't ever try to mess with me,
Else you won't even get a chance to apologise.

Don't consider me to be weak and fragile,
As I remain to be invincible,
A free soul with twinkling eyes,
Who always believes in godly miracles.

If I believe you to be my lucky charm,
I'll protect you from any havoc,
But if betrayed,
You may regret making me run amuck.

Holy Love

My love for you is as pure as a white feather
Soft, silvery, pious and elegant,
Devoid of ephemeral pleasures,
It's symbolic of spiritual union.
Far from the bewitching worldliness,
It often gives me a sense of completeness.
Sometimes I get stuck in wordiness...
Fail to express but you feel it
I get ecstatic.
Your silence makes me cry,
I die to hear from you
As if waiting since my birth.
I feel like clinging to you
But you depart ruthlessly,
Leaving me with the devils
Vicious, venomous, holding back to bite.
I pray to God to save my soul from getting
stained,
To be united with you forever.

Your holy presence makes me speechless
I feel numb, breathless,
But you rejuvenate me with your tender touch
I gasp and feel alive,
Hoping to be with you till eternity...

An Oath

I hear Death singing a choir in my ears,
I was horrified but not surprised.
I witnessed umpteen succumbing to its call,
Willingly or unwillingly, everyone reaches the
same destination,
It's not a novel phenomenon.
I still recall the trauma, the agony of losing my
mother,
I still cry in pain to get her back from the
heavenly abode,
To make her cherish each moment of life,
To fulfill all her desires but nothing helps
She is gone....gone forever,
Not to come back but to make me realise what I
missed,

The distance, the void created, can never be
filled.
But suddenly I see people around me,
Still wanting my love, my time
How can I ignore them?
How can I be so cruel?
I can't give up living for those who left,
I'll live for those who need me.
The sun still shines to keep us warm
To let us feel that we exist even now.
We will keep breathing,
Not to die erratically
But to enlighten and uplift others.

Unconquerable

Oh life!
I bleed profusely!
Cheated by the devils,
I feel betrayed.
Hiding their faces,
They stabbed me from the back.
Before falling unconscious,
I heard Lucifer laughing,
As if teasing me,
Enjoying my agony,
Forcing me to take extreme steps,
Without knowing my inner strength,
The power of my prayers,
That heals me within no time.
I feel alive, ready to fight,
Not the face but the force.
The small ants,
Trying to harm me finally give up,
I relish the silence before symphony,
Proclaiming me to be invincible.

Buffoons

Recently I came across a group of cravens,
Gossiping, pampering each other,
Living in an unconscious state,
Suffering from mental disorders,
Without realising the ultimate truth of life,
One blind, supporting another blind.
Whenever I hear their feeble cries of pain,
I feel pity for them.
They might die without realising
The rationale behind their existence,
I wonder... is this what people live for?
To be one among a crowd of buffoons,
Who are busy digging their own graves,
From where they will never see the celestial
light,
But it's too late to awaken these nincompoops,
Who feel elated to be captives,

Dancing to the tunes of others,
They dwell in the abode of the dead,
To rest eternally in an inferno.

Angel

An angel resides beyond any anguish,
Rising from its own ashes,
It lives till eternity.
A living spirit,
Striving to create 'the Land of the leal',
It pushes people to be the ultimate conqueror,
Having vision more than sight,
It adores all but connects with none.
Being blessed with a peculiar sense of seeing the
naked truth,
It possesses the power to control demons.
Emerging victorious,
It perpetually rules the city-of-light,
Leading a spiritual life,
It becomes immortal.

Heavenly Union

Surrounded by the divine power I feel great,
It gives me immense pleasure
Asif nothing can ever harm me,
The sacred moment touches my soul,
I feel like dying.
Having seen all I feel elated,
Nothing appeals to me,
But the purity of heart,
An incarnation of Divinity
Makes me ecstatic.
I crave for blessings,
To be one with the Almighty,
To live beyond the fear of death,
Power, Pelf, Position,
All become immaterial.

I see the hidden truth of life,
The only reason behind my existence
Is a hope for the heavenly union.

Futile Quest

I often wonder why people go for a 'futile quest
of love',
When they fail to understand what it means,
Love for some equals to physical gratification,
Something sensational that evokes carnal
appetite,
For me, it's spiritual,
A sacred river of holy water.
Here arises a conflict:
Is love a sensual merriment or
A heavenly pleasure where one sacrifices all?
In my view, love reflects the purity of heart,
It is the heavenly union of two souls,
Not the climax of passionate emotions,
But the beginning of a novel era,
Where you forget yourself and become one with
the other,
Love never separates; it only unites.
One who calls it a 'Divine Sin' is undoubtedly
mistaken,
Love is the virtue of nobles,
It is not the touch, passion or lust that arouses,
It is the holiness of heart that appeals.
Not governed by the plethora of desires,

I prefer to be confined to the four walls of my
temple,
For me, these four walls symbolise Niyam,
Saiyyam, Vrat and Tapasya,
A hedonistic person can never fathom how it
feels,
But the platonic love remains perpetual,
Love is not hypocrisy,
It is immortality;
Endless, pious and spontaneous.

Born Benefactor

I remain invincible and unbreakable,
Not because of power or pelf,
But because of my inner strength.
It motivates me not only to excel
But to be humane,
To cherish the sweet moments of life,
Though short-lived but immortal in my memory.
I seek solace,
Not from an outer source but from within.
Even in my dreams, I expect nothing from others
Because I know deep down in my heart
That I am destined to give others,
A born benefactor,
Blessed to be benevolent.

Art of Life

Suffering is an inseparable part of our lives,
But to smile in distress is the art of life.
Only few could ever excel in this art,
Gifted with an incredible power,
To fight and never succumb.
I've gradually learned to smile in pain,
May it be physical or mental,
Because it always teaches me
An undying lesson of life,
I repeatedly forgive those who make me suffer,
And move forward,
To read a new chapter of life…
My closest ones have often deceived me,
Leaving me in endless agony,
But I revive swiftly,

Without allowing satanic forces
To overshadow my resilience,
I fight constantly not only to survive
But to be triumphant.
Sometimes I grow tired of playing
This game of hide-and-seek
As I wish to dwell eternally
In the heavenly abode
Where no one can ever betray me,
And I rest peacefully
To get the treasure trove of happiness.

Dev: A Living Hope

My cherubic angel,
An incarnation of Divine,
Soothing, comforting,
Rushing breathlessly on my simplest call,
Putting his tireless efforts to make me smile,
Succoring me innocently to forget the torments
of life,
Making my days special with his sublime
presence,
Awaiting my homecoming
with his twinkling eyes,
Wiping away my tears with his tender hands,
Trying his best not to let me cry,
Bringing me overwhelming joy,
While experimenting new recipes
to satisfy my hunger,
Inspiring me to live, to smile
Even in distress.
Enabling me to cherish even the flavourless food
of life,

Appealing me to love even in betrayal… The list remains endless
But I don't feel sorry for this interminable effusion,
As my heart knows no limits
When it speaks of him.
Sometimes I wonder,
What I would do
While departing this ephemeral world,
Leaving him behind,
My heart feels heavy.
But then I stand still,
Pondering over life's blessings,
Thanking the Almighty
For bestowing upon me
The precious gem
I don't regret any vacuum,
Created out of chaos,
When I witness my life
Filled with the heavenly presence of my little bundle of joy,
I wish I could live eternally with my shining Sirius
Who fills my life with the sacred light,
Even if I die today,
I'll have no regrets
As I feel content with my living hope.

Child of God

Recently I came across
A child of God who touched my heart,
Speaking softly, guiding, motivating,
Showing me the path of truth,
The ultimate paragon,
Whispering into my ears,
I wonder how someone can be
So innocent, so simple,
Untouched by all the vices,
A saint disguised as an educator,
Loving, caring, sacrificing,
So selfless, so sweet,
Even failing the sweetness of sugar,
My mind refuses to accept
The presence of a godly person
But my heart silently whispers,

Urging me not to trust my mind but my instincts,
To believe in what my eyes, my ears witness,
A blessing in disguise,
Sent from the heaven
To free me from all sufferings,
To make me feel
The presence of the Divine.

Desire

I often wonder,
How could I forget to sing a holy hymn?
To behold the beauty of nature?
To fly and to try?
To cherish the blessings of life?
The questions remain endless and unanswered,
Caught in the spider's web
I forgot to even smile …
To live and enjoy has become tales of the past…
I no longer smile but only calculate
expenditures,
And the monthly EMIs.
I walk on the deadly road of life
That leads nowhere.
Living the life of a nomadic,
I regret my mistakes,
But all in vain,
For the Wheel of Time never turns back,

Leaving us with no opportunity to regret or
reconstruct,
But I feel resolute to turn the Wheel of Fortune,
To relive and rejoice,
Not for my own self
But for those around me,
Who look at me with hope.
I'll never let their hope die
Rather I'll give them wings to fly in the sky,
To behold and touch the rainbow of life,
And to live perpetually in El Dorado.

Lonely Wanderer

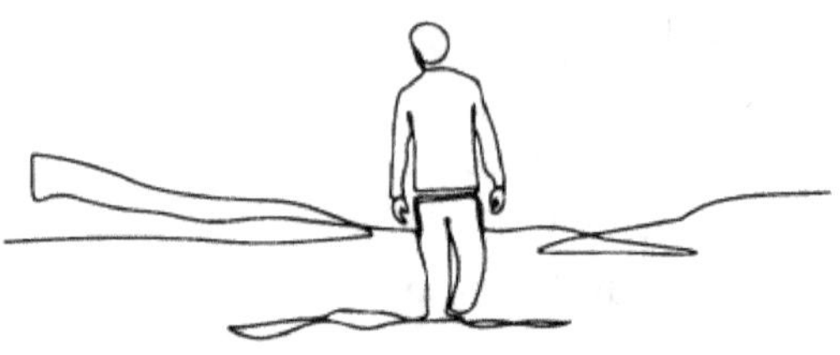

In the tumultuous tempest, I tread alone,
On this cimmerian night, my heart turns to
stone.
While lovers find solace in caressing embrace,
I wander deserted in this enshrouded expanse.

Torrential rain echoes my heart's refrain,
Nostalgia grips me with bitter disdain.
I deferred my dreams for future flights,
Now regrets pour down with the rain tonight.

Darkened dungeons mirror my abysmal pain,
As I ponder the cost of life's mundane.
I curse myself for snubbing each moment, each
kiss,
Now drowned in the storm, in this tenebrous
abyss.

Each drop a tear, each gust a sigh,

In the storm's fury, abandoned I cry.
No shield from tempest, no hand to hold tight,
Just memories haunting in the squalls' might.

I mourn inconsolably in tempestuous showers,
Lost in regrets, amid eclipsed hours.
O, forsaken love, adrift amidst the rain,
Grant me absolution, bring sunshine again.

Myriad Shades of Life

Life is an enigma swathed in shadows,
A manuscript of arcane dialects,
A crucible wherein one's essence glows,
The forge in which one's spirit's mettle checks.

Life is a symphony, ethereal,
Its harmonies, an echo in the soul,
A bridal veil, its secrets lyrical,
Awaiting hands to lift its mystic toll.

Life, a Sisyphean quest profound,
Where mortals strive against fate's unyielding
tide,
A mountain range where peaks and vales
abound,
A tale of valour, sung with stoic pride.

Life, a miracle in death's embrace,
A dawn's ephemeral glow, with dusk in sight,
Laughter's chorus through a youth's bright gaze,
A painter's palette, splashed with pure delight.

In myriad forms, life composes perennial
melodies through the zither,
Yet in its twilight, timeless threnodies find its
rhythm.
Life, a tapestry both grand and grim,
Woven by threads of fate, through light and dim.

That One Glance

Amidst rain's veil, whispers softly sway,
Echoes from dark clouds, hearts in disarray.
Tears cascade ceaselessly, from the eyes'
embrace,
Yet today, no ear heeds the heart's tender grace.

Those bygone memories, solace do impart,
Yet no one sings a new melody to my heart.
Raindrops transmute to tears, falling bold,
Stormy tempests, heart's resolve unfold.

For that one glance I yearn, my heartstrings
entwined,
In balmy air, thirst for love is defined.
Cold night's playful tease, stirs the soul's chord,
Once more, a call echoes, love adored.

Monsoon clouds hover, heart's ache anew,
Lost love's absence, deeply I rue.
Lips softly hum an ancient refrain,
In rain's embrace, thirst for him sustains.

Lost in the labyrinth of fate, where tears silently
fall,
Memories of laughter fade, as darkness
enshrouds all.
Yet amidst despair's relentless tide, a fragile
ember glows,
A testament to resilience, as sorrow ebbs and
flows.

Indian Queen

I came across an Indian Queen,
Magnificent and miraculous,
Fascinating like the serene shadows of silver
moon,
Gazing at her was a celestial boon.

Draped in blue attire,
Beneath the sun's golden veil,
I saw her sitting with ultimate grace.

Her twinkling eyes sparkled,
Whispering the secrets unsaid,
Her sacred lips sang hymns to a Divine
mermaid.

Her aura, a radiant miracle,
Her gaze, an enchanting spell,
A testament of beauty and strength,
Her elegance was enough to captivate hearts.

She gleamed like a constellation,
Her voice, a lyre in a temple,
Her words, symphonies of the divine,
She miraculously succeeded in capturing the
heart of mine.

I got hypnotised listening to her symphony,
Her footsteps wove the tapestry of harmony.
Unfailingly I witnessed the Royalty in her blood,
She was forgiving and pious like a blooming
bud.

An angel adorned in jewels with a diamond
heart,
She is my muse, always on guard.

Caravan

Alone, I am a wanderer adrift in the galaxy's compound,
Where stars weave tales of existence, both elusive and profound.
In solitude, I ponder my place, my past a haunting specter,
How did I, a misfit soul, ascend amidst celestial splendour?

Among luminous constellations ablaze with cosmic lore,
How did this lowly star chart its celestial course?
Deep within, gratitude swells for the enigmatic force,
That lifted me from terrestrial depths to celestial heights,

Binding me to the eternal dance of twinkling
lights.

In perpetual shimmer, indebted to the unseen
force,
Guardian of stars, bestowing a timeless grace,
Guiding the caravan of luminaries through
boundless space,
I remain a humble wanderer in the celestial
embrace.

Solitary Beacon

In the echoing hollows, I stand,
Where trust crumbles to dust in trembling hands.
Betrayed by kin, in the depths I roam alone,
In solitude, I weep, with no one to call home.

In this cruel theater of feigned empathy,
Where hearts turn cold, devoid of sympathy,
Hope, a distant specter, fades to black,
Lost in the abyss, I struggle to backtrack.

Yet amidst the shadows, a flicker remains,
A resolve born from relentless pain.
No longer seeking solace in another's embrace,
But forging ahead, alone in this grace.

In the cacophony of greed and need,
Even millionaires beg and plead,
When it comes to extending a supporting hand,
I see no one willing to take a stand,
Amidst the darkness of the night, I am the
solitary light,
Guiding lost souls through their plight.

Though agony grips and despair holds tight,
I'll stand, battered but unbroken, in the fight,
To be the voice in the silence, the unwavering
plea,
A solitary beacon of hope in this sea of misery.

Alone In The Crowd

Amidst the multitude, I am an apparition,
An ephemeral wraith in a sea of indifferent
souls.
No tender heart perceives my presence
Or senses the depths of my anguish.

My gaze, laden with unshed tears, surveys the
throng,
Finding no solace but the omnipresent specter of
despondency,
That ensnares and devours my spirit.

In vain, I endeavor to stifle the torrent of my
emotions,

Yet the tears cascade unbidden, an unrelenting
deluge.
My eyes seek the suitor who abandoned me to
this desolate crowd,
To endure the harrowing solitude that gnaws at
my psyche.

Bereft and tormented, I am ensnared,
By the agonising reality of my isolation,
The stark realisation that I stand solitary amid a
sea of humanity.
My lament, silent yet piercing, is a testament to
the cruelty and apathy
That surrounds me—every face a mask of
dispassion,
Each person, a thrall to their insatiable desires.

Confronted by these demons of indifference,
I am suffused with the stark and bitter
understanding,
Of what it truly means to be alone in a crowd.
In the end, the relentless tide of despair sweeps
me away,
Consumed by the inexorable darkness,
My spirit, crushed beneath the weight of a
callous world.

Hermit

I encountered a reclusive sage,
Humble yet resolute,
His voice intoning sacred hymns,
His aura, a blinding force against adversaries,
He transcended the material realm,
Even fear itself recoiled before him.
Witnessing his popularity, envy inflamed the
hearts of many,
Who sought to denigrate his repute.
They vented their frustrations,
Through relentless verbal assaults.
They spared no effort,
To tarnish his image before the masses,
Manipulating the credulous.
They endeavored to usurp his influence,
Maligning and pursuing him tirelessly,
To unravel his arcane secrets,
All to no avail.
Thus, they convened a council,
A conclave of venomous serpents,
To plot his eternal silence.
But the hermit, perceiving their malevolent
schemes,
Remained unperturbed despite the peril.
In his tranquil silence lay his fortitude.

He invoked the Divine,
Interceding for the welfare of the populace,
Unconcerned for his own preservation.
His supplications reached celestial ears,
Miraculously transforming minds,
Illuminating truth to the deceived.
Their clandestine plot was uncovered,
Revealing the malefactors.
The populace, recognising their folly,
Renewed their fidelity,
Reinstating the sage's venerated status,
Living henceforth in harmony,
Under the aegis of the hermit.

Mysterious Light

While witnessing the velvet canvas of night,
I find myself frightened in the depths of night,
A symphony of silence weaves a cryptic sweep,
Where terrifying shadows dare to creep.

Engulfing darkness and starlight intertwine,
In the ravine of the sublime,
A crimson thread through the abyss,
I stand aghast to see the cosmos bleed.

A silent cry, a mournful gleam,
Often haunts me in my dreams,
Each apparition sings a silent song,
Of people forgotten, ages long.

Nebulous whispers swirl in the cosmic sea,
Holding my breath I strain to see,
In the ghastly expanse a mysterious light,
Colors in the dark sky on an immortal night.

Silence

In silence lies my strength,
Confrontation evades my tongue,
Strength emerges unspoken.
Even in isolation, I don't feel alone,
For my silence accompanies,
Paving the way for my success.

Blessing me with the power to weave words,
Creating wonders destined for immortality.
Silence makes me powerful,
I feel ready with an indomitable weapon,
Capable of triumph in catastrophic conflicts.

Emerging victorious,
It never feels proud,
Savouring its conquest in silence,
Capturing not only hearts but also souls.

A wellspring of energy
Bestowing upon me tranquility and equilibrium,
I feel a surge of vigor
Like the Greek Goddesses,
Armored yet serene.
Poised to conquer,
To inscribe the chronicles of success.

Commitment

Don't panic, my love,
Your protection is my vow.
I urge you not to see yourself as a liability,
For you are my cherished responsibility.

My little angel, my heartbeat, my world,
I wish you to dwell eternally in the fabled land.
I promise to stand by your side with unwavering
devotion,
As I have no hidden expectations.

When I extended my hand to shield you,
I knew the hardships I would face,
But I took it as a challenge,
An opportunity to win the race.

You are a miraculous creation of Divinity,
And I am just a humble devotee,
Always remember that I am not bound by my
commitment,
But my offering to the Almighty.

My words are my bond, unbreakable and true,
I'll risk my life to always shield you.
So, fear not, and drift into sleep,
Let my lullaby guide you where dreams run
deep.

Dance to the heavenly tunes, carefree and light,
Until my last breath, none shall bring you fright,
For I stand here to guard and protect you
Through dooming days and darkened nights.

Sleep peacefully, my dearest and think not of
gloom,
For my blessings will forever surround you.
As long as the stars shine and the moon glows
bright,
My love will shield you through day and night.

Lost Hope

While waiting for you,
I realise the weight of years,
My vision fading,
Yet still hoping to see you return.
My heart beats with the fragile hope of reunion.

My hair, once a cascade of perfume,
Now turning grey, losing its luster.
Chasing your shadow, I wander in solitude,
Losing warmth, but still breathing,
Yearning to hear your footsteps at my door.

With each passing moment, my body grows
colder,
My lips turn pale in your absence.
I cry out, but my voice is swallowed by silence.
As the clock ticks, fear grips me,
Doubting our reunion.
I question my existence without you.

Like a corpse wandering in a desolate land,
I peer through the darkness,
Finding no comfort for my weary soul.
I regret each moment spent chasing illusions.

Desperately, I call your name,
But you remain deaf, absorbed in your pursuits.
I weep, I repent, I wither away, etching in the
sand,

'Return while I still breathe,
For no love can be kindled on a pyre.'

Chamber of Secrets

I have a small cell,
A sanctuary where I do as I please.
It's my creative haven,
My chamber of secrets,
Witnessing my desires,
Shaping my ideas,
Creating miracles.

Darkness never follows me there;
It's fully illuminated
With my positive energy.
I love my small cell,
Wish to dwell there forever.

It knows who I truly am;
I don't need to wear a mask.
It helps me explore myself,
Revealing the best in me.
It shows me my beautiful reflection,
Supporting my aspirations.

I can dream there undisturbed,
Its rhythm, in sync with my heartbeat.
It never misguides, always praises,
Inspiring me to be at my best.
I wish everyone had a magical chamber,
To propel them forward in life.

Godfather

I decided to extend a supporting hand,
Because I know well,
The agony of being left alone in a crowd,
The pain of having no one by your side when
you need them most.
I understand the heartache of being ignored by
people close by,
Left stranded with no one to console you when
you cry out in despair.
I know the torment of feeling isolated even
around your soulmate,
The crushing sense of purposelessness
That makes you question the value of your own
life.

I've sought saviors but found only devils,
Felt the sting of humiliation as those I trusted
disowned me,
And the sting of inferiority for lacking the
means to spend lavishly on others.
There came a time when the cruelty of
venomous creatures became unbearable,
And the thought of eternal rest seemed like the
only escape.
I know the pain, the shame and the sufferings

That neither let you live nor let you die in peace.
This understanding compelled me to extend a
supporting hand
To those who are searching for a Godfather
amidst the feigning crowd.